EVOLATIO   D1649436

ION

AND

THE HORSE!

BY

Chris Moller

THESE NEW HOOVES
ARE KILLING ME!

J. A. ALLEN

BRITISH LIBRARY CATALOGUING IN PUBLICATION DATA
A CATALOGUE RECORD FOR THIS BOOK IS AVAILABLE
FROM THE BRITISH LIBRARY

ISBN 0-85131-564-X

PUBLISHED IN GREAT BRITAIN BY
J.A.ALLEN & COMPANY LIMITED
1, LOWER GROSVENOR PLACE,
BUCKINGHAM PALACE ROAD, LONDON SWIW OEL

PRINTED IN GREAT BRITAIN BY
THE LONGDUNN PRESS LTD, BRISTOL

FOREWORD

OF ALL THE RELATIONSHIPS BETWEEN MAN AND ANIMAL, THE ASSOCIATION OF MAN AND THE HORSE HAS UNDOUBT-EDLY BEEN THE MOST SIGNIFICANT IN ALL OF EVOLUTION. TO PUT IT IN A HORSE-NUT SHELL, WITHOUT THE HORSE HOW COULD WE HAVE THE HORSELESS-CARRIAGE?

AS WELL AS ARCHEOLOGICAL EVIDENCE FROM PERSIA, INDIA, ASSYRIA AND EGYPT WE CAN SEE FROM EARLY CHINESE RECORDS THAT THE HORSE OFFICIALLY BEGAN HIS ASSOCIATION WITH MAN IN 2637 B.C. THUS MAKING THE MODERN HORSE 4629 YEARS OLD!

THE HORSE BEGAN LIFE 55 MILLION YEARS AGO WHEN HE WAS CALLED EOHIPPUS, WAS ONLY TWELVE INCHES HIGH AND REGARDED AS A TASTY SNACK BY MOST OF THE OTHER CREATURES THAT WERE AROUND AT THE TIME.

OVER THE NEXT 54 MILLION YEARS LITTLE EOHIPPUS CONCENTRATED ON HIDING AND THINKING OF WAYS OF KEEPING HIMSELF OFF THE MENU.

HE CAME DOWN OFF TIP TOES , GOT HIMSELF SOME HOOVES , GREW A BIT AND PRACTISED LIKE MAD AT OUTRUNNING ALL HIS HUNGRY NEIGHBOURS .

HE ALSO CHANGED HIS NAME SEVERAL TIMES , FINALLY SETTLING ON EQUUS BEING MUCH SHORTER THAN HYCOTHERIUM, MESOHIPPUS , PLIOHIPPUS OR DELICIOUS .

A MILLION YEARS AGO WHEN HE FIRST CLAMBERED DOWN FROM THE TREES MAN THE HUNTER IMMEDIATELY BECAME AN EQUUS LOVER.

HE EVEN PUT UP PICTURES OF THE EQUUS ON HIS LIVING-ROOM WALL.

THEN IN 2637 B.C. MAN JUST HAPPENED TO CATCH AN EQUUS AND DISCOVERED THAT IT WAS REALLY QUITE FRIENDLY AND PREFERRED MAN TO SIT ON IT RATHER THAN EAT IT.

AND AT LAST MAN HAD FOUND THE KEY TO SUCCESSFUL EVOLUTION. HE FOUND THAT HE COULD NOW RUN AWAY FROM DISAGREEMENTS WITH DISAGREEABLE NEIGHBOURS ON HIS NEW FRIEND 'HORSE' MUCH QUICKER THAN ON HIS OWN.

AND HE DISCOVERED THAT HORSE'S STRENGTH ENABLED IT TO PULL ANYTHING THAT TOOK MAN'S FANCY.

AT LAST MAN WAS ABLE TO KEEP UP WITH HIS DOMEST-ICATED WOLVES, WHEN SEEKING OUT THE RAIDERS OF HIS STOCK AND CROPS. THIS GIVES US THE FIRST EXAMPLE OF HUNT-ING ALTHOUGH THE QUARRY WOULD HAVE BEEN MORE VARIED THEN.

IN FACT MAN WAS SO TAKEN WITH HIS NEW PARTNER THE HORSE THAT HE WAS NOT ABOVE SHOWING OFF THEIR NEWLY ACQUIRED SKILLS TOGETHER, INVENTING IN THE PROCESS THE CIRCUS RING.

AFTER ALL THE EFFORT OF GETTING THESE STONES HERE, IT SEEMED A BIT OF A WASTE JUST TO USE THEM ON MID-SUMMER MORNING!

WITH ALL THIS INVENTING GOING ON IT WAS SURPRISING THAT, HAVING INVENTED THE WHEEL, IT SHOULD TAKE THE FATHERS OF CIVILISATION SUCH AS THE SUMERIANS QUITE SOMETIME TO PUT THE WHEEL AND THE HORSE TOGETHER EFFECTIVELY.

I STILL THINK WE SHOULD THINK ABOUT PUTTING THE WHEELS ON THE BASKET

MUMMY!

BUT EVENTUALLY THE EVER-WILLING HORSE FOUND HIMSELF REPLACING THE ILL-TEMPERED AND AWKWARD ONAGER OR WILD ASS IN THE SHAFTS OF THE HEAVY SOLID-WHEELED WAGONS.

BUT THERE WERE STILL PROBLEMS TO BE IRONED OUT, SUCH AS A HARNESS THAT PREVENTED THE HEAVY WAGON OVER-RUNNING THE HORSE ON STEEP HILLS.

BY 1500 BC THE HITTITES HAD SOLVED MOST OF THESE WEIGHTY PROBLEMS WITH KIKKULIS'S COMPREHENSIVE SET OF INSTRUCTION TABLETS DEALING WITH ALL ASPECTS OF MAN'S ASSOCIATION WITH THE HORSE-THE FIRST MANUAL OF HORSEMANSHIP

WHICH COVERED NOT ONLY THINGS SUCH AS FEED, WATER, EXERCISE, BUT ALSO GROOMING, BEDDING AND EVEN IN-CLUDED INSTRUCTIONS FOR MUZZLES TO PREVENT CRIB-BITING.

ALTHOUGH, LIKE MANY ACCIDENTAL DISCOVERIES, IT COULD WELL HAVE BEEN CRIB-BITING THAT LED TO THE NEXT MAJOR DEVELOPMENT, THE LIGHTWEIGHT BODY AND SPOKED WHEELS OF THE WAR CHARIOT.

THE NEW SPOKED WHEELS WERE FITTED WITH INDEPEND-ENT AXLES TO MAKE THEM MORE MANOEUVRABLE AND QUICKER TO TURN ROUND IN TIGHT SPOTS.

THE CHARIOT SOON TURNED UP AS FAR AFIELD AS INDIA AND CHINA AS WELL AS ASSYRIA WHERE IT SOMETIMES CARRIED THREE OR EVEN MORE.

I SHALL BE GLAD WHEN THE NOVELTY OF THE CHARIOT WEARS OFF!

BUT BY AND LARGE IT CARRIED TWO. IN CELTIC LANDS, WHERE THEY SCORNED CLOTHING IN BATTLE, THE CHARIOT WAS OPEN AT THE FRONT, AS WELL AS AT THE BACK AND PRESUMABLY WAS MOSTLY USED FOR THE 'FULL FRONTAL' ASSAULT.

GET THAT SHIELD UP? YOU MUST BE JOKING!

ALTHOUGH MUCH HOTTER IN ASSYRIA AND EGYPT THEY WORE CLOTHES AND PUT 'DASHBOARDS' ON THE FRONT (SINCE MAN HAS ALWAYS BEEN ILLOGICAL). HERE THE KING OR PHAROAH WIELDED THE SPEAR AND BOW AND LEFT THE DRIVING TO A DRIVER.

IN EGYPT PHAROAH WAS ONE OF THE FIRST TO USE CHARIOTS IN MASSED RANKS BUT WAS UNLUCKY ENOUGH TO RUN UP AGAINST (OR SHOULD IT BE INTO) THE WORLD'S FIRST COURSE-BUILDER TO INCLUDE A WATER HAZARD — MOSES !

WITH (THEREBY SETTING THE PATTERN FOR WATER-HAZARDS DOWN THE AGES) PREDICTABLE RESULTS.

AS WELL AS THE DISAPPOINTING MARKS SCORED BY THE CHARIOT AT THE WATER-HAZARD IT WAS ALSO LIMITED AS TO WHAT OTHER OBSTACLES IT COULD TACKLE.

SO THAT EVERYBODY THAT DIDN'T WANT TO BE CONQUERED (AND MADE TO PUT UP PYRAMIDS AND SUCH) BUILT LARGE WALLS TO KEEP THE CHARIOT OUT.

THIS MADE THE CHARIOT LARGELY OBSOLETE FOR WARFARE (EXCEPT IN CHINA AND INDIA WHERE THEY OBVIOUSLY HADN'T HEARD ABOUT MOSES OR PYRAMIDS) AND IT WAS RE-ASSIGNED TO CARRYING MESSAGES AND IMPORTANT PEOPLE.

IN MORE PEACEFUL TIMES IT WAS ALSO VERY IMPORTANT AS THE CENTREPIECE OF THE GAMES WHERE EVERYBODY CAME TO RELAX, HAVE FUN AND BET ON THE OUTCOME OF THE CHARIOT RACES.

UNFORTUNATELY FOR THE HORSE THEY TOOK THEIR BETTING VERY SERIOUSLY AND IF IT WAS A 'FUNERARY'GAMES THE LOSERS OFTEN ENDED UP ACCOMPANYING THE LATE KING TO MEET THE GODS IN PERSON.

IN CHINA HOWEVER THEY WERE MORE CONSIDERATE OF THE HORSE'S FEELINGS, MAKING VERY LIFELIKE TERRACOTTA STATUES OF THE HORSE AND BURYING THOSE INSTEAD.

IN GREECE, WHERE THE CHARIOT WAS LESS POPULAR BECAUSE OF THE MOUNTAINOUS TERRAIN, THEY HAD REALISED THAT THERE WAS A LOT MORE TO THE HORSE THAN JUST PULLING A CHARIOT OR BEING BURIED.

A VERSATILITY WHICH WAS WELL DEMONSTRATED AT THERMOPYLAE :
WHEN HARD-PRESSED BY THEIR ENEMIES THE GREEKS MOVED THEIR
HORSES SIDEWAYS , MAKING THE NARROW PASS EVEN NARROWER,
INADVERTENTLY PERFORMING THE FIRST DRESSAGE MOVEMENT.

THE TOTAL LACK OF SUCCESS OF THIS MANOEUVRE AND THEREFORE
OF THE BATTLE UNDOUBTEDLY HAS A LOT TO DO WITH THE UNPOPUL-
ARITY OF DRESSAGE BUT HAPPILY DIDN'T PUT THE GREEKS AND
THE HORSE OFF THE IDEA OF THE USE OF CAVALRY.

ONE OF THE REASONS FOR THE GREEKS CONTINUING ENTHUSIASM FOR CAVALRY LAY WITH THEIR 'CHEF D'EQUIPE' XENOPHON WHO HAD WORKED FOR THE OPPOSITION, THE PERSIANS, AND WHO WAS THEREFORE ABLE TO GIVE THE GREEKS THE LOW-DOWN ON THEIR DEADLY ENEMIES.

XENOPHON ALSO WROTE AN IMPORTANT 'HORSEY BOOK' WHICH IS IN FACT STILL FOLLOWED RELIGIOUSLY TODAY. IT COVERED EVERYTHING OF IMPORTANCE LIKE FEEDING AND MUCKING OUT.

IT POINTED OUT ALL THE BASIC ESSENTIALS OF HORSEMAN-SHIP LIKE THE IMPORTANCE OF TREATMENT OF THE HORSE'S MUZZLE, OF AVOIDING A HARD MOUTH AND ENCOURAGING ACCEPTANCE OF THE BIT.

SINCE MUCH OF THE EXISTING SADDLERY HAD BEEN PASSED ON FROM THE CHARIOT, XENOPHON DETAILED NEW IDEAS FOR TACK AND INTRODUCED THE CIVILISED WORLD TO THE 'SNAFFLE' OR JOINTED METAL BIT.

AND HE EVEN INVENTED A NEW TECHNIQUE FOR HARDENING THE HORSE'S HOOVES BY STANDING THE HORSE ON A PILE OF STONES.

ENCOURAGED BY ALL THIS IMPROVEMENT THE GREEKS DE-CIDED THAT IT WAS TIME TO GO AND TEACH 'THE ART OF HORSEMANSHIP' TO THE PERSIANS.

WHICH GAVE THE NEW HEAD OF THE GREEK STATES THE MACE-
DONIAN PRINCE ALEXANDER THE CHANCE TO GET ON HIS 'HIGH-
HORSE' AND GO AND MAKE A NAME FOR HIMSELF.

THE PRINCIPAL OF THE 'HIGH HORSE' WAS TO MAKE SURE
THAT A GENERAL WAS WELL ENOUGH MOUNTED TO BE VISIBLE
TO HIS MEN AND THEREFORE INSPIRE THEM DURING THE MELÉE
OF BATTLE.

ALEXANDER'S 'HIGH HORSE' WAS CALLED BUCEPHALUS MEANING BULLHEAD, EITHER ON ACCOUNT OF THE BRAND ON HIS SHOULDER OR FROM HIS FIERCE AND IMPOSING APPEARANCE PARTICULARLY ON THE BATTLEFIELD.

BUT FIERCE OR NOT BUCEPHALUS WAS VERY FAITHFUL, AND HAVING FIRST BEEN RIDDEN BY ALEXANDER AS A BOY, WOULD ONLY ALLOW HIM ON BOARD AND WAS REPUTED TO BE EXTREMELY JEALOUS IF ALEXANDER WENT NEAR ANOTHER HORSE.

HAVING LEARNT FROM XENOPHON OF THE FEARSOME MOUNTED BOWMEN OF THE STEPPES, THE PARTHIANS AND SCYTHIANS, ALEXANDER IMMEDIATELY SHOWED HIS OUTSTANDING GENERAL-SHIP BY PERSUADING THEM TO CHANGE OVER TO HIS SIDE.

A MANOEUVRE WHICH LEFT HIM FREE TO TAKE PERSIA, SYRIA, PHOENICIA, EGYPT, IRAN, BITS OF INDIA AND ANYTHING IN THE EAST THAT WASN'T NAILED DOWN, THEREBY INTRODUCING THE INHABITANTS TO THE JOYS OF CIVILISATION.

THE SUCCESS OF ALEXANDER AND BUCEPHALUS LED TO ALL KINGS AND GENERALS GETTING ON 'HIGH HORSES' SO THAT THEY COULD HAVE A BETTER CHANCE OF GETTING TO THE TOP AND IN-CIDENTALLY GET A BETTER VIEW OF THE PROGRESS OF THE BATTLE.

AND THE BENEFITS THAT THIS SPREAD OF CIVILISATION BROUGHT -PARTICULARLY TO ALEXANDER- WERE NOTED BY THE ROMANS WHO IMMEDIATELY SET OUT TO PERSUADE ALL THEIR NEIGHBOURS THAT THEY WOULD LIKE TO BE 'CIVILISED' TOO.

THE ROMANS TOO HAD A PROMINENT CHEF D'EQUIPE BUT WHO APPARENTLY WASN'T AS GOOD AS XENOPHON SINCE HE WAS CALLED SECUNDUS (OR SECOND) AND HE EVEN HAD SOME RATHER STRANGE IDEAS ON THE NATURAL HISTORY OF THE HORSE.

THIS LACK OF EXPERTISE RESULTED IN THE ROMAN CAVALRY AT FIRST BEING TREATED AS MERELY AN EXTENSION OF THEIR FORMIDABLY DISCIPLINED AND WELL-DRILLED LEGIONS.

WHILST THESE TACTICS WERE MORE THAN GOOD ENOUGH TO PERSUADE THE GAULS AND OTHERS TO EMBRACE CIVILISATION THE CARTHAGINIANS DEFINITELY WEREN'T TOO KEEN ON THE IDEA AND PRODUCED THEIR SECRET WEAPON—THE ELEPHANT.

THIS WAS INITIALLY VERY SUCCESSFUL AND THE ROMANS WERE FORCED (BY SEVERAL DEFEATS IN A ROW) TO RE-ORGANISE THEIR CAVALRY INTO SEPARATE SQUADRONS WHERE THEIR SPEED COULD BE USED TO OUTFLANK THEIR MORE CUMBERSOME OPPONENTS.

THIS NEW EMPHASIS ON CAVALRY RATHER THAN MOUNTED INFANTRY FINALLY ENABLED THE ROMANS TO PERSUADE THE CARTHAGINIANS TO BECOME CIVILISED AND TO RAZE CARTHAGE TO THE GROUND TO SHOW THERE WERE NO HARD FEELINGS.

IT ALSO ENABLED THE ROMANS TO INTRODUCE THE 'BARB' INTO WESTERN EUROPE, AN ARAB HORSE LONG ADMIRED FOR ITS QUALITIES OF SPEED, INTELLIGENCE AND STAMINA OVER GREAT DISTANCES.

TO KEEP IN TOUCH WITH ALL THIS NEW CIVILISATION THE
ROMANS BUILT LOTS OF STONE-PAVED ROADS.

THESE ALWAYS STRAIGHT HARD ROADS GAVE THE CHARIOT A NEW
LEASE OF LIFE, AS IT COULD BE USED WITH RELAY TEAMS TO
OPERATE A REGULAR LONG-DISTANCE SERVICE CARRYING MAIL
AND PASSENGERS.

IN THE WILDER PARTS OF EUROPE THE WAR-CHARIOT STILL ENJOYED POPULARITY THANKS TO THE DEVELOPMENT OF HUGE WHEELS TO COMPENSATE FOR THE STATE OF THE NON-EXISTENT ROADS,

AND THE LARGE SCYTHES ON THE AXLES WHICH THE LIKES OF QUEEN BOUDICCA INTENDED TO BE THE WEAPON THAT WOULD GIVE HER AN 'EDGE' OVER THE ROMANS WHEN THEY CAME TO CIVILISE BRITAIN.

WITH THE DEATH OF THE GREAT ALEXANDER, THE GRECIAN CIVILISATION ESTABLISHED BY HIM IN THE EASTERN MEDITERRANEAN BEGAN TO CRUMBLE,

LEAVING THE WAY APPARENTLY WIDE OPEN FOR THE ROMANS TO EXPAND EASTWARDS. UNFORTUNATELY THE PARTHIANS HADN'T BEEN SHOWN THE SCRIPT AND SNEAKILY ONLY CAME CLOSE ENOUGH TO SHOWER THE ROMAN CAVALRY WITH ARROWS, THEN RIDE OFF AGAIN

NEEDLESS TO SAY THIS DEFEAT CAUSED THE ROMANS TO HAVE A MAJOR RE-THINK, TO INVENT MAIL ARMOUR FOR THEIR CAVALRY AND JUST IN CASE THIS STILL DIDN'T WORK THEY TOO BRIBED THE PARTHIANS TO JOIN THEM AS MERCENARIES.

THE NEW ARMOUR (AND THE BRIBERY) WORKED SO WELL THAT FINALLY THE ROMANS WERE ABLE TO LEAVE THE FIGHTING TO THEIR MERCENARY MERCENARIES AND ALL RETIRE TO ROME TO BE DECADENT EVEN TO THE EXTENT OF ACCEPTING A HORSE AS THEIR EMPEROR.

NATURALLY NEWS THAT THE ROMANS WERE DECLINING ALL OVER THE PLACE SOON SPREAD AS FAR AS THE MASTER-HORSEMEN OF THE STEPPES, THE HUNS. THEY WERE ALWAYS INTERESTED IN CIVILISATION —ESPECIALLY WHEN IT WAS WEAK AND FULL OF THE BETTER THINGS IN LIFE.

GATHERING A FEW HUNDRED THOUSAND FRIENDS, ATTILA SET OFF FOR ROME TO CLAIM HIS SHARE OF THESE GOOD THINGS, LUCKILY FOR THE ROMANS THE HUNS WEREN'T INTERESTED IN CONQUERING THEM ('CIVILISING' THEM) — JUST RAIDING THEM.

UNDERSTANDABLY, WHEN THE ROMAN MERCENARIES CAUGHT SIGHT OF THE HORDES OF HUNS BREASTING THE RISE IN FRONT OF THEM THEY DECIDED ON SOME FAIRLY RADICAL STEPS.

THE HUN 'RAID' THEREFORE LEFT A HOLE IN THE ROMAN DEFENCES THAT YOU COULD MARCH AN ARMY OF GOTHS THROUGH – OR VISIGOTHS, OR OSTROGOTHS, OR VANDALS – ALL OF WHOM DID JUST THAT TO TAKE OVER ANYTHING THAT THE HUNS HADN'T BEEN INTERESTED IN.

THIS ULTIMATE DEFEAT OF THE ROMANS AND THE FALLING-OUT OF THE GOTHS ETC. OVER THE LOOT, EFFECTIVELY PUT THE LIGHT OF CIVILISATION OUT IN MOST OF EUROPE FOR AGES, WHICH IS WHY IT BECAME KNOWN AS THE DARK AGES.

WITHOUT CIVILISATION TO UNITE THE MYRIAD TRIBES INTO GREAT ARMIES (AND SO CONDUCT MAJOR WARS) EVERYBODY WENT HAPPILY BACK TO FIGHTING EVERYBODY ELSE IN SCORES OF MINOR WARS.

BUT LUCKILY SINCE ALL EVOLUTION DEPENDS ON CONFLICT OF A KIND – ANY KIND! – EVEN IN THE DARKNESS OF EUROPE THE PARTNERSHIP BETWEEN THE HORSE AND WARRING MAN GREW EVER CLOSER,

AND MANY OF THE GREAT ADVANCES OF CIVILISATION WERE RETAINED. ADVANCES SUCH AS THE MORE EFFECTIVE USE OF THE MOUNTED WARRIOR, THE LONG SPEAR FOR KEEPING THE INFANTRY RESPECTFUL AND THE IRON OR MAIL VEST IN CASE THEY STILL WEREN'T.

ELSEWHERE IN THE WORLD THE CHINESE HAD PUT UP A GREAT WALL TO KEEP OUT THE HUNS. THIS HAD WORKED SO WELL THAT IT HAD BEEN QUICKER FOR THE HUNS TO RAID ROME THAN RIDE ALL THE WAY ROUND FIFTEEN HUNDRED MILES OF WALL.

BEHIND THIS GREAT WALL LAY THE FORBIDDEN CITY WHERE NO ONE WAS ALLOWED TO GO, AND WHERE WAS BRED THE 'HEAVENLY' HORSE, A FABLED HORSE THAT WAS SUPPOSED TO SWEAT BLOOD.

AND WHERE THEY HAD PRODUCED SOMETHING THAT WAS TO HAVE A HUGE IMPACT ON THE FIGHTING MAN AND HIS HORSE (PARTICULARLY WHEN THEY CAME WITHIN RANGE) — GUNPOWDER!

IN INDIA THEY ALSO HID BEHIND A WALL WHICH WAS A BIT HIGHER THAN THE GREAT WALL BUT LUCKILY FOR THE INDIANS DIDN'T HAVE TO BE BUILT—THE HIMALAYAS. THERE, LARGELY SAFE FROM THE 'STEPPES LIGHT HORSE', THE ELEPHANT STILL HELD SWAY

BACK IN EUROPE THE FRANKISH KING, CHARLES, FINALLY RE-KINDLED THE LIGHT OF CIVILISATION BY THE SIMPLE EXPEDIENT OF CONQUERING ALL HIS NEIGHBOURS LIKE THE SAXONS, MAYGARS ETC. AND MODESTLY DECLARING HIMSELF EMPEROR CHARLEMAGNE OR CHARLES THE GREAT.

BUT AS WELL AS ACQUIRING HIMSELF THE NEW HOLY ROMAN EMPIRE HE ALSO ACQUIRED TWO THINGS THAT WERE TO BE CRUCIAL TO EVOLUTION, CIVILISATION AND EVERYTHING. FROM THE AVARS CAME THE STIRRUP, AND FROM THE MOORS THE SADDLE.

MEANWHILE, IN BRITAIN, EVERYONE WAS INDULGING IN THE NATIONAL PASTIME OF SQUABBLING WITH EACH OTHER AND CREATING LEGENDS TO COVER UP THEIR UNCIVILISED BEHAVIOUR. LEGENDS OF UTHER PENDRAGON, OF ARTHUR AND THE SWORD EXCALIBUR.

ACCORDINGLY ARTHUR'S BRITAIN BECAME POPULATED WITH WIZARDS, HOLY RELICS, MAIDENS IN DISTRESS AND SHINING-ARMOUR-PLATED KNIGHTS ALL POSITIVELY OOZING CHIVALROUS AND COURTEOUS BEHAVIOUR.

THE TRUTH HOWEVER WAS VERY DIFFERENT AND EVEN THE FAMOUS TABLE WOULDN'T HAVE BEEN ROUND, IT JUST APPEARED TO BE – GOING ROUND AND ROUND AND ROUND . . .

EVEN ALFRED DID NOT SPEND HIS TIME SITTING AROUND BURNING CAKES, HE WAS TOO BUSY ORGANISING THE FIRST RACES FOR REWARD (AS A WAY OF DISTRIBUTING A DEAD MAN'S GOODS) WHICH LED TO THE HORSE BEING SPECIALLY BRED FOR SPEED.

ARTHUR'S FABLED KNIGHTS WERE IN FACT LITTLE ADVANCED FROM THE ROMAN CATAPHRACT OR MAILED TROOPER, FAR TOO BUSY FOR JOUSTING AND DAMSELS IN DISTRESS, BUSY FENDING OFF ATTACKS FROM ANGLES AND SAXONS,

AND FROM JUTES (WHO DIDN'T INVENT THE RUG), IRISH PICTS, FELLOW BRITONS AND IN PARTICULAR ATTACKS FROM THE GREATLY FEARED SEA-WOLVES, THE NORTHMEN OR VIKINGS.

THE VIKINGS FULLY APPRECIATED THE VALUE OF CAVALRY FOR THEIR LIGHTNING RAIDS AND CARRYING BOOTY BACK TO THEIR LONGSHIPS, AND BRED A SMALL STURDY PONY THAT WAS HAPPY TO TRAVEL WITH THEM ACROSS THE NORTHERN SEAS.

AND THOSE VIKINGS WHO SETTLED 'NORTHMAN'S LAND' OR NORMANDY AND BECAME NORMANS USED THIS SKILL TO GREAT EFFECT IN 1066 WHEN, AS WE ALL KNOW, HISTORY REALLY STARTED.

WHEN MATILDA HAD FINALLY COMPLETED THE BAYEUX TAPESTRY IT SHOWED US THAT ALTHOUGH IT WAS AN ARCHER THAT PROVED TO BE ONE IN THE EYE FOR HAROLD, IT WAS THE NORMAN SHIP-BORNE CAVALRY THAT TIPPED THE BALANCE IN THE BATTLE OF HASTINGS.

AND AS SOON AS WILLIAM HAD ELIMINATED THE OPPOSITION HE SET ABOUT CIVILISING BRITAIN BY LETTING ALL THE LAND TO HIS BARONS AND INVITING ALL THE RESIDENTS TO BECOME SERFS —THE FEUDAL SYSTEM.

THE KEY TO THE SUCCESS OF THE NORMAN CIVILISATION LAY IN THE HORSE THAT WILLIAM RODE AT HASTINGS. THE ANDALUSIAN WAS NOT ONLY LARGE ENOUGH TO BE A 'HIGH-HORSE' FROM WHICH THE LORDS COULD KEEP THEIR SERFS ON THE STRAIGHT AND NARROW,

IT WAS ALSO STRONG ENOUGH TO CREATE A NEW ROLE FOR ITSELF ON THE BATTLEFIELD — THE WARHORSE. A ROLE IT WAS TO FULFILL ON MANY A LONG AND ARDUOUS CAMPAIGN AND ABOUT WHICH IT WAS TO HAVE MANY A TALE TO TELL . . .

THE WARHORSE DID NOT IN FACT HAVE TO BE MASSIVE IN ORDER TO CARRY THE ARMOURED FIGHTING MAN, A SHORT BACK AND STRONG TENDONS WERE THE ESSENTIALS, ALONG WITH SOLID BONE.

BUT IT WAS OBVIOUS TO THE NORMANS THAT THE GREATER THE SIZE OF THE HORSE THE GREATER WOULD BE ITS IMPRESSION ON THE INFANTRY.

ALL THE GREAT HORSE'S NATURAL AGGRESSION WAS EN-COURAGED TO MAKE HIM INTO A FORMIDABLE WEAPON IN HIS OWN RIGHT, EVEN DOWN TO EQUIPPING HIS FRONT HOOVES WITH PROTRUDING STUD-LIKE NAILS.

AS A FURTHER REFINEMENT, THE KNIGHT, SECURE IN DEEP SADDLE AND STIRRUP, COULD COUCH A MUCH LARGER LANCE UNDER HIS ARM AND USE THE FULL WEIGHT OF THE GREAT HORSE TO MAKE SURE THAT EVERYONE 'GOT THE POINT'.

ALL THIS LED TO THE DEVELOPMENT OF STRONGER 'PLATE' ARMOUR TO GIVE BETTER PROTECTION TO RIDER AND HORSE, ALTHOUGH THE ADDITIONAL LAYERS OF METALWORK MUST HAVE BROUGHT A WHOLE NEW MEANING TO BEING 'UP TO WEIGHT'.

AND FINALLY, RESPLENDENT IN ELABORATELY DECORATED 'POT-HELM', BREASTPLATE, CUISSE AND GAUNTLET FOR THROWING DOWN, THE KNIGHT AND HIS GREAT HORSE OR 'DESTRIER' EM-ERGED TO USHER IN THE TRUE AGE OF CHIVALRY.

CHIVALRY WAS LARGELY ABOUT SHOWING OFF ALL THE KNIGHT'S FINERY, TRAPPINGS AND SKILLS IN FRONT OF THE LADIES AND IMPRESSING THE POPULATION WHEN GOING OFF TO WAR AND RE-TURNING IN TRIUMPH.

SO WHEN, SURPRISINGLY PERHAPS, THERE WERE NOT MANY WARS ABOUT THE 'JOUST' WAS INTRODUCED TO GIVE CHIVALRY THE OPPORTUNITY TO CARRY ON IMPRESSING THE POPULATION AND VYING FOR THE LADIES' FAVOURS.

ALTHOUGH CHIVALRY COULDN'T HAVE BEEN VERY CHIVALROUS IN THE HEAT OF BATTLE, VERY STRICT RULES WERE IMPOSED IN THE JOUST. SUCH AS STAYING ON THE DEXTER OR RIGHT SIDE OF THE BARRIER (WHICH SAVED COLLIDING WITH THE ONCOMING METALWORK).

AND, IMPORTANTLY FOR THE HORSE'S ENJOYMENT OF THE JOUST, IT WAS DECLARED A HEINOUS FOUL TO TOUCH AN OPPONENT'S DESTRIER WITH LANCE, MACE, SWORD ETC. PUNISHABLE BY IMMEDIATE BANISHMENT BELOW THE SALT AND BEYOND THE PALE.

BUT SUCH WAS THE IMPORTANCE OF CHIVALRY (FIGHTING) TO CIVILISATION THAT THE DESTRIER HAD EVOLVED INTO A TYPE OF HORSE THAT COULD ONLY BE USED FOR ONE PURPOSE —FIGHTING!

LUCKILY FOR THE DEVELOPMENT OF THE HORSE SUCH AN AGGRESSIVE ARISTROCRAT, LIKE THE KNIGHT HIMSELF, REQUIRED A HOST OF FOLLOWERS TO PERFORM ALL THE MUNDANE TASKS AND LEAVE HIM FREE TO SPEND ALL HIS TIME FIGHTING.

FIRST IN THE LINE WAS THE PALFREY, THE FORERUNNER OF THE PACER, WHICH COULD ACCELERATE TO TOP SPEED WITHOUT BREAKING STEP OR 'CHANGING GEAR' AND WHICH THE KNIGHT USED WHEN NOT ACTUALLY IN ACTION.

NEXT CAME THE ROUNCY, RIDDEN BY THE KNIGHT'S SQUIRE AND SHIELD-BEARER, THIS WAS THE VERSATILE COB OF MEDIEVAL TIMES, SHORT IN THE LEG, BROAD IN THE BEAM AND PLACID OF NATURE.

THE COURSER WAS THE SPEED MERCHANT OF THE STRING, THE MEDIEVAL RACEHORSE USED BY HERALDS AND OTHER MESSENGERS FOR PASSING ON VITAL INFORMATION.

LAST, BUT CERTAINLY NOT LEAST, CAME THE SUMPTER OR CAPUL CARRYING THE ARMOUR, WEAPONS, SPARES, CHANGES OF CLOTHING BANNERS, TENTS, BANQUET PLACE SETTINGS, PARADE TACK, FOOD, GRAIN, AND ALL THE OTHER LITTLE ESSENTIALS OF CHIVALRY.

TO SAVE THE CHIVALRY OF EUROPE FROM BECOMING BORED WITH JUST MINOR SCRAPS AND JOUSTING, THE INFIDELS CONSIDERATELY TOOK OVER THE HOLY LAND WHICH GAVE THE KNIGHTS AN IDEAL EXCUSE TO PACK THEIR CAPULS AND SET OFF TO GET IT BACK AGAIN.

APART FROM GETTING A LASTING TASTE FOR PACKAGE HOLIDAYS TO THE SUN, EUROPE'S MORE PONDEROUS HEAVY ARMOUR SOON CAME TO APPRECIATE THE SPEED AND AGILITY OF THEIR MORE LIGHTLY-ARMED OPPONENT'S ARAB HORSES.

THE CRUSADERS BECAME VERY KEEN ON ACQUIRING THEM FOR BREEDING PURPOSES. NO DOUBT, SINCE ALL THE DESTRIERS WERE STALLIONS AND THE SARACEN'S MOUNTS WERE ALL MARES, THE HORSE WAS NOT UNHAPPY ABOUT THIS ARRANGEMENT.

IN ANSWER TO THE EASTERN BOWMEN THE CRUSADERS HAD PRODUCED THEIR OWN ARTILLERY, THE 'ARBALEST' OR CROSS-BOW, WHICH THE SARACENS DIDN'T LIKE BECAUSE THE BOLTS WENT STRAIGHT THROUGH THEIR LEATHER ARMOUR.

WHILE EUROPE WAS BUSY TRYING TO 'CIVILISE' PALESTINE THE 'STEPPES LIGHT HORSE' GATHERED ONCE MORE. THIS TIME IT WAS THE MONGOLS UNDER GENGHIZ KHAN. THEY HAD THE REPUTATION OF SPENDING THEIR ENTIRE LIVES IN THE SADDLE - OR ALMOST.

THEY FOUND THEIR WAY ROUND CHINA'S GREAT WALL, 'LIBERATED' THE 'HEAVENLY HORSES' FROM THE IMPERIAL STABLES AND SET THEM TO WORK IMPROVING THE QUALITY OF THEIR OWN HERDS (THEY ALSO TOOK OVER CHINA).

UNDER BABER THE MONGOLS ALSO WENT ROUND INDIA'S
WALL, THE HIMALAYAS, TO ESTABLISH THE MOGUL CIVILISATION
AND ACQUIRE YET MORE BLOODSTOCK FOR THEIR HERDS (NOT
THE ELEPHANTS) WHICH WERE BEGINNING TO BE QUITE SUPERIOR.

AND UNDER TAMERLANE 100,000 OF THEM REACHED AS FAR AS
HUNGARY, BUT SINCE THEY HAD AT LEAST 20 HORSES EACH,
EASTERN EUROPE SOON BECAME GRAZED OUT AND HORSE-
SICK AND THEY ALL HAD TO TURN ROUND AND GO HOME.

AND SO THE REST OF EUROPE BREATHED A HUGE SIGH OF RELIEF AT NOT HAVING TO FIGHT THEM AS WELL — OR PROVIDE GRAZING FOR ALL THOSE HORSES — SIGNED A TRUCE WITH SALADIN AND WENT HOME THEMSELVES.

ALTHOUGH EUROPEAN ARMOUR WAS EFFECTIVE AGAINST THE SARACEN BOW AND EVEN THEIR OWN CROSSBOW, THE ENGLISH HAD DEVELOPED THE 'LONGBOW' WHOSE ARMOUR-PIERCING QUALITIES HAD SUPPOSEDLY BEEN WELL TESTED BY ROBIN HOOD'S MERRY MEN.

ANDSO, THINGS BEING VERY QUIET ON THE HOME FRONT EDWARD THE BLACK PRINCE (FOLLOWED BY HENRY V) DECIDED TO GO AND TEST THE NEW FIREPOWER AGAINST THE FRENCH (BEING THE CLOSEST).

THE LONGBOW WAS A PRECURSOR OF FUTURE FIREPOWER AND WAS WIELDED ON FOOT FROM BEHIND SHARPENED STAKES TO KEEP THE FRENCH KNIGHTS AT ARROW'S LENGTH, AND, BEING ON FOOT, THE ARCHERS DIDN'T MIND THE GROUND BEING A BIT BOGGY.

THE IMPACT OF THE LONGBOW WAS TO MAKE EUROPE LOOK AGAIN AT A LIGHTER AND MORE MOBILE CAVALRY, A CAVALRY THAT COULD AVOID BEING BOGGED DOWN OR SHOT UP – OR BOTH.

THE FRENCH EVEN PRODUCED A MUCH LIGHTER LEADER WHO WAS NOT ONLY (HORROR OF HORRORS!) A WOMAN BUT ALSO IN-CIDENTALLY A GOOD GENERAL. THINKING THIS TO BE UNFAIR AND NOT LIKING TO BE BEATEN BY A WOMAN, THE ENGLISH WENT HOME.

BY THIS TIME JOUSTING WAS LOSING POPULARITY, SO IN ENGLAND THE DUKE OF YORK STARTED A CIVIL WAR TO RELIEVE THE BOREDOM, WHICH BECAME KNOWN AS THE WARS OF THE ROSES.

THIS WAS NOTABLE, ACCORDING TO THE IMMORTAL BARD WM. SHAKESPEARE, AS THE NEAREST ENGLAND CAME TO EMULATING THE ROMANS AND HAVING A HORSE ON THE THRONE.

IN SPAIN THEY WERE STILL BUSY TRYING TO GET MORE 'ARABS' AND 'BARBS' FROM THE MOORS, WHO DIDN'T WANT TO PART WITH THEM – OR SOUTHERN SPAIN. IN BETWEEN WHILES THEY ALL PRACTISED LIKE MAD TILTING AT WINDMILLS.

WHEN, FINALLY, THEY PERSUADED THE MOORS TO PART WITH SOME OF THEIR HORSES – AND SOUTHERN SPAIN, THE SPANISH SENT CORTES AND THE HORSES ON A LONG AND INVIGORATING SEA-CRUISE.

IN THE COURSE OF THIS CRUISE, CORTES BUMPED INTO MEXICO AND LOST NO TIME IN INTRODUCING THE NATIVES, THE AZTECS, TO THE BENEFITS OF CIVILISATION AND THE CORRECT WAY TO SHOW GRATITUDE.

DESPITE BEING HUGELY OUTNUMBERED CORTES WAS ABLE TO CIVILISE ALL OF MEXICO SINCE THE AZTECS HAD NEVER SEEN A HORSE BEFORE, AND THOUGHT THAT HORSE AND RIDER WERE ONE BEING.

THE AZTECS PROVED TO BE SO GENEROUS THAT THE SPANISH SENT PIZARRO TO CIVILISE THE INCAS, AIDED ONCE MORE BY THE HORSE AND, LIKE CORTES, BY THE MUSKET, ALTHOUGH THE EARLY MUSKET WAS USED MOSTLY FOR DRAMATIC EFFECT.

IMPORTANTLY FOR THE EVOLUTION OF THE HORSE IN THE AMERICAS NOT ALL OF THE CONQUISTADOR S' MOUNTS RETURNED TO SPAIN, SOME GOT LOST, SOME STRAYED AND SOME, PERHAPS, WERE INADVERTENTLY LEFT BEHIND.

AND WHEN THESE 'CASTAWAYS' FOUND THE GREAT GRASS-
LANDS OF BOTH NORTH AND SOUTH AMERICA THE SUCCESS OF
THE 'MESTENGO' OR MUSTANG WAS GUARANTEED.

THE SPANISH MUSKETS WERE A DEVELOPMENT OF THE CANNON
BROUGHT TO EUROPE FROM CHINA BY YET MORE OF THE HORSEMEN
OF THE STEPPES, THE TARTARS, BUT AS YET ITS ACCURACY AND RELIABILITY
LEFT A LOT TO BE DESIRED, EVEN AGAINST STATIONARY TARGETS.

WHEN THE TARTARS FINALLY GOT BORED AND WENT HOME, ONE OF THEIR TRIBES, THE TURKS, DECIDED TO BECOME EUROPE'S NEW NEIGHBOURS, BUT NOT KNOWING HOW TO BE GOOD NEIGHBOURS, WERE RELUCTANT TO DO ANY TRADING, PARTICULARLY OF THEIR SUPERB HORSES.

IN ENGLAND MEANWHILE HENRY VIII HAD SEPARATED TROUBLESOME SCOTS FROM THEIR CLAYMORES, TROUBLESOME WIVES FROM THEIR HEADS AND TROUBLESOME ABBOTS FROM THE MORAL DILEMMA OF THEIR OPULENT LIFESTYLES (AND FROM THEIR MONASTERIES)

HE ALSO BEGAN A TREND FOR USING THE HORSE FOR MORE CIVILISED PURSUITS OTHER THAN WAR TO OCCUPY THE INCREAS- ING AMOUNTS OF LEISURE TIME AVAILABLE , GENTLE PERSUITS SUCH AS HUNTING ,

AND FALCONRY WHICH FOUND GOOD USE FOR THE NOW RE- DUNDANT KNIGHT'S PALFREY , WHOSE EASY-GOING GAIT WAS ESSENTIAL FOR NOT RUFFLING THE FEATHERS OF THE FEAR- LESS FALCON .

THE CAPUL, USED TO CARRYING BAGGAGE, NOW CARRIED THE LADIES AND PERHAPS SOME LIGHT REFRESHMENT OUT TO SEE THE SPORT IN THAT FORERUNNER OF THE CARRIAGE, THE LITTER

AND THE COURSER WAS READIED FOR ITS ROLE AS A RACE-HORSE AT THE ROYAL STUD AT TUTBURY BY THE IMPORTATION OF GONZAGA STOCK FROM PADUA, THE DESCENDENTS OF WHICH WERE TO BECOME KNOWN AS THE ENGLISH THOROUGHBRED.

THE DESTRIER HAD HAD A VERY QUIET TIME OF THINGS FOR SOME WHILE, APART FROM BEING USED AS A 'HIGH HORSE' BY GOOD QUEEN BESS AS SHE ENCOURAGED HER NAVY TO CONTINUE TO KEEP ENGLAND'S SHORES FREE OF EUROPEANS,

UNTIL THAT ESSENTIAL OF CIVILISATION, THE CIVIL WAR BROUGHT BACK DEMAND FOR ITS FIGHTING SKILLS. THIS TIME IT WAS CROMWELL WHO NEEDED THE WARHORSE FOR HIS SUPERBLY DRILLED BUT SLIGHTLY PONDEROUS MUSKET-WIELDING TROOPERS OR 'DRAGOONS'.

AND KING CHARLES NEEDED IT TO CARRY HIS FLAMBOYANT STILL-PART-ARMOURED 'CHEVALIERS' OR CAVALIERS, ALTHOUGH IT HAS TO BE SAID THAT DESPITE ITS WEIGHT THE ARMOUR WAS NOT NOW MUCH USE IN STOPPING MUSKET, LET ALONE CANNON, BALLS.

SO WHILE THE ROYALISTS FAVOURED THE BREEDING OF A LIGHTER AND FASTER WAR-HORSE, CROMWELL AND HIS PARLIAMENTARIANS STUCK TO THE MORE SOLID AND DEPENDABLE TYPES.

NO SOONER HAD THE VARIOUS BREEDING PROGRAMS GOT INTO FULL SWING THAN THIS CIVIL WAR CAME TO AN INCONSIDERATE END WITH DEFEAT FOR THE BRAVE AND FEARLESS CAVALIER.

IN EUROPE HOWEVER, WHERE WARS WERE MUCH MORE POPULAR, THE LIGHTER WAR-HORSE'S SPEED AND MOBILITY WAS FOUND TO BE ESSENTIAL AGAINST THE COSSACKS, TURKS (WHO STILL WOULDN'T TRADE) EACH OTHER, AND THE INCREASING AMOUNTS OF ORDNANCE FLYING ABOUT.

THIS SUCCESS WAS TO LEAD TO THE FORMATION OF SOME OF THE MOST FAMOUS REGIMENTS OF HORSE: THE CUIRASSIERS, HUSSARS AND ULANS, WHILE THE HEAVIER WAR-HORSE WAS REDUCED TO PULLING THE CANNON.

THE RELATIVE PEACE IN ENGLAND HAD ALLOWED NATIVE BREEDS TO DEVELOP HAPPILY FROM THEIR SAXON AND VIKING ORIGINS; BREEDS SUCH AS THE NEW FOREST, THE WELSH, AND OF COURSE THE GARRON, WHICH CARRIED THE SCOTS ON THEIR CROSS-BORDER RAIDS.

THERE WAS EVEN A NATIVE, THE RHUM PONY, WHICH WAS NOT HAIRY AT ALL. IT HAD SHED ITS COAT AND RELIED SOLELY FOR PROTECTION ON AN EXCEPTIONALLY THICK SKIN. THIS PROBABLY HAD NOTHING TO DO WITH THEIR LONG ASSOCIATION WITH THE SCOTS.

THE FINAL DEFEAT OF THE SCOTS AT CULLODEN AND THE IMPOSITION OF ENGLISH CIVILISATION ON THE HIGHLANDS (BY THE BANNING OF THE TARTAN AND THE PIPES AND THE CLEARANCE OF ALL THE HIGHLANDERS TO MAKE WAY FOR SHEEP)...

...LED MANY SCOTS TO LOOK TO THE NEW WORLD. JOINED BY REFUGEES FROM THE EUROPEAN WARS AND OTHERS WHO HAD LITTLE CHOICE, THEY SET OFF, TAKING ONLY THEIR FINEST STOCK SINCE SPACE ON THE SHIPS WAS AT A PREMIUM,

THUS INTRODUCING THE HORSE BOTH TO AUSTRALIA AND NEW ZEALAND AND THE USE OF THE HORSE TO NORTH AMERICA; ALTHOUGH THE WILD MUSTANG WAS NOW COMMON, IT WAS THESE SETTLERS THAT SHOWED THE INDIAN HOW USEFUL THE HORSE COULD BE.

AND AS THE SETTLERS' WAGGONS SPREAD WESTWARD SO THE HORSE OR 'MEDICINE DOG' TRANSFORMED THE LIVES OF THE PLAINS INDIANS WHO CAME TO PRIZE THE NEW ACQUISITION ABOVE ALL ELSE,

AND WHO LOST NO TIME IN CATCHING UP WITH THEIR ANCESTORAL COUSINS FROM THE STEPPES IN THE ART OF HORSEMANSHIP.

IN EUROPE THE ADVANCE OF CIVILISATION WAS DEMANDING MORE AND BETTER COMMUNICATIONS, AND ROADS WERE BEING RE-ESTABLISHED —ALTHOUGH THE SURFACES WERE NOT INITIALLY BACK UP TO THE STANDARD OF THE FAMOUS ROMAN ROADS.

SINCE ONLY THE HEAVIER VEHICLES COULD HOPE TO SURVIVE ON THESE INDIFFERENT SURFACES, A NEW ROLE WAS FOUND FOR THE DESTRIER, LARGELY REDUNDANT NOW THAT THE DAYS OF CHIVALRY WERE OVER.

BUT TRAVEL WAS STILL VERY SLOW AND THE HEAVY HORSE-DRAWN VEHICLES WERE LITTLE IF ANY FASTER THAN THE OX-DRAWN GOODS WAGGONS AND THE PACKHORSES.

ANDSO, SINCE MORE SPEED IS ALWAYS THE GOAL OF CIVILIS-ATION, THE ROADS WERE IMPROVED ; AND SINCE CIVILISATION IS ALSO ALWAYS COST CONSCIOUS , THE TRAVELLER FOUND HIMSELF (AND HERSELF) BEING INVITED TO CONTRIBUTE .

TO TAKE ADVANTAGE OF THESE BETTER ROADS (AND ALSO TO GET VALUE FOR THEIR TOLL MONEY) THE MUCH LIGHTER HUNGARIAN 'KOCSI' OR COACH WAS INTRODUCED WHICH EVEN BOASTED METAL SPRINGS FOR THE ADDED COMFORT OF THE PASSENGERS.

PACE AND NOT JUST PULLING POWER WAS NOW REQUIRED OF THE HORSE AND THE OLD 'ROUNCY' WAS PREFERRED TO THE PONDEROUS GREAT HORSE, HAVING A BETTER TURN OF SPEED BUT STILL SUFFICIENT STRENGTH TO COPE WITH THE NEW COACH.

THIS MORE CIVILISED MEANS OF TRANSPORT ALLOWED THE GENTRY TO VISIT THEIR ESTATES MORE FREQUENTLY, AND HENCE TO DEVELOP THEIR FARMS AND STUDS WHICH HAD FOR GENERATIONS BEEN SOLELY DEVOTED TO SUPPLYING WAR-HORSES FOR THE MILITARY.

WITH ENGLAND'S PEACE ENSURED BY HER NAVY THE REDUNDANT WAR-HORSE WAS ALSO ADAPTED FOR OTHER MUNDANE TASKS ONCE PERFORMED BY THE OX, TASKS LIKE HAULING AND PLOUGHING, AND SOON THE CLASSIC WORKHORSE, THE 'OLD ENGLISH BLACK' EMERGED.

THE EVENTUAL CIVILISING OF SPAIN AND TURKEY HAD AT LAST ALLOWED EUROPE TO ACQUIRE SUFFICIENT OF THE GREAT 'BARB' AND 'TURK' SIRES TO COMPLETE THE BLOOD-LINES THAT WOULD SO EXPAND THE EVOLUTION OF THE HORSE.

AND ALTHOUGH MUCH OF EUROPE STILL NEEDED THE OLD WAR-HORSE FOR WAR, AND THE LEISURELY ACTIVITIES OF THE GENTRY IN FRANCE HAD BEEN 'CUT SHORT' BY THE REVOLUTION, THERE WERE STILL AREAS WHERE THE 'FRESH BLOOD' WAS GREATLY IN DEMAND.

NAPOLEON EVEN ESTABLISHED SPECIAL ARAB STUDS OR 'HARAHS' TO PROVIDE HIM WITH THE MOUNTS HE NEEDED FOR CIVILISING THE REST OF THE WORLD BUT THESE WERE STILL SOLELY CONCERNED WITH PRODUCING A BETTER WAR-HORSE FOR HIS EVER-EXPANDING CAVALRY.

SO IT WAS IN PEACEFUL ENGLAND THAT THE GREAT EVOLUTION TOOK PLACE. THE GENTRY, HAVING PUT THE HEAVY HORSE TO WORK COULD CONCENTRATE ON PRODUCING THE PERFECT HORSE FOR HIS VARIOUS LEISURE ACTIVITIES.

WHETHER AT WAR OR PLAY THE HORSE WAS STILL THE ULTIMATE STATUS SYMBOL AND THEREFORE CRUCIAL TO CIVILISATION - ALL THE MORE SO BECAUSE IT EPITOMISES SPEED.

AND WHERE BETTER TO START THAN WITH THE MOUNT OF THE MESSENGER, THE FLEET-FOOTED 'COURSER', SO THAT THE GENTRY COULD PIT THEIR BEST AGAINST THOSE OF THEIR PEERS (ON RACE – 'COURSES') AS ONCE THEY PITTED CHAMPIONS IN COMBAT.

THE INTRODUCTION OF 'BLOOD' SUCH AS THE GODOLPHIN AND DARLEY ARABS, CURWEN'S BARB AND THE BYERLY TURK WERE SO SUCCESSFUL THAT THE GENERAL STUD BOOK WAS STARTED SO THAT THE LINEAGE OF ALL QUALITY HORSES COULD BE TRACED AND PROVEN.

AND THE THOROUGHBRED HAD PROPERLY ARRIVED, ITS PEDIGREE ENSURING ITS EXCLUSIVITY AND THEREFORE THE PRESTIGE OF THE OWNER — TO SAY NOTHING OF THE EXORBITANT PRICES THAT COULD BE CHARGED FOR ITS PROGENY.

IN THE ABSENCE OF ANY WARS, THE GENTRY LOOKED AROUND FOR OTHER DIVERSIONS AND SETTLED ON HUNTING. SO THE ROUNCY WAS THE NEXT TO RECEIVE THE ATTENTIONS OF THE THOROUGH-BRED STALLION, TO PRODUCE THE PERFECT HUNTER.

WITH ALL THE IMPROVEMENTS IN CARRIAGE DESIGN THERE WAS ALSO A DEMAND FOR A FASTER MORE SHOWY HARNESS HORSE FOR WHICH THE NEW-LOOK ROUNCY PROVED TO BE EQUALLY AS GOOD-LOOKING (AND HAPPY) ON THE ROAD AS THE HUNTING FIELD.

THE HACKNEY, THE TROTTING HORSE, HAD FOR A LONG TIME BEEN A LIGHT RIDING HORSE, BUT WAS ABOUT TO BECOME CONFUSED. HE HAD NOT BEEN CONSIDERED SUITABLE FOR LADIES UNTIL AN IMPROVED SIDE-SADDLE ALLOWED THEM TO RIDE THE TROT WITH DECORUM.

BUT AS SOON AS THE HACKNEY HAD SETTLED TO THIS DECOROUS AND DECORATIVE ROLE, IT WAS DECIDED THAT HE WOULD BE EVEN BETTER DISPLAYED IN THE SHAFTS OF THE NEW SMALL CARRIAGES LIKE THE GIG.

THIS COMMANDEERING OF THE LADY'S HACK WAS NOT HOWEVER A BAD THING SINCE IT LED TO A MUCH GREATER DIVERSITY OF THE HUNTER WHICH BECAME EQUALLY AS HAPPY GENTEELY DISPORTING ITSELF WITH THE SIDE SADDLE AS CHARGING ACROSS COUNTRY WITH A RED-BLOODED MALE.

STRANGELY THE PALFREY, WHICH, WITH ITS EASY-GOING GAIT WOULD HAVE BEEN IDEAL FOR THE LADIES, HAD ALL BUT DISAPPEARED FROM EUROPE ONLY TO MYSTERIOUSLY RE-APPEAR IN AMERICA TO BE-COME THE FAVORED FRIEND OF THE COWBOY.

ALL THESE ADVANCES LED TO A GREAT INCREASE IN GENERAL TRAVEL. FOR THOSE WHO COULDN'T AFFORD THEIR OWN COACHES AND WHO CHOSE NOT TO RIDE, SCHEDULED SERVICES WERE ESTABLISHED, TRAVELLING 'STAGES' OF 50 MILES PER DAY AND RESTING OVERNIGHT AT INNS.

HOLD IT DOWN IN THERE! — SOME OF US HAVE TO WORK IN THE MORNING!!

AND WITH FURTHER IMPROVEMENTS TO THE ROAD SURFACE (WITH THE INVENTION OF TARMAC) THE CREAM OF THESE SERVICES CARRIED THE ROYAL MAIL AND WERE GIVEN PRIORITY OVER ALL OTHER ROAD USERS, CLEARING THE PATH WITH A DEAFENING BLAST ON THE COACHMAN'S HORN.

NOW !!

THE MAIL COACHES WERE STRICT ABOUT SEGREGATING THE 'INSIDE' OR FIRST CLASS PASSENGERS, FROM THE IMPECUNIOUS 'THIRD' CLASS, WHICH HAD TO HANG ONTO THE OUTSIDE NO MATTER WHAT THE WEATHER.

BUT WITH THE MAILS AND THE PAMPERED INSIDE PASSENGERS THERE WERE NOW RICH PICKINGS APLENTY ON THE HIGHWAYS AND THE DASHING AND GLAMOROUS FIGURE OF THE 'HIGHWAYMAN' APPEARED EVERYWHERE UTTERING HIS BLOOD-CURDLING CRY.

THERE WAS EVEN A PARSON WHO LOOKED TO SUPPLEMENT HIS, TO HIM, MEAGRE STIPEND BY TAKING HIS COLLECTION PLATE OUT ONTO THE ROADS OF SOUTHERN ENGLAND.

IT'S NOT THE LURKING I MIND SO MUCH, IT'S HAVING TO LISTEN TO HIM PRACTISING HIS SERMONS!

AND THERE WERE OTHER 'GENTLEMEN OF THE ROAD' WHO WERE NOT SO MUCH INTERESTED IN THE PASSENGERS AS THE MUCH-IN-DEMAND HIGH-QUALITY HORSE THAT TRANSPORTED THEM.

I SAY! WHAT'S THE BLASTED HOLD UP NOW?

HORSE STEALING BECAME BIG BUSINESS AND WAS HIGHLY ORGANISED. A HORSE WOULD BE STOLEN IN THE NORTH BY A MOUNTED 'PRIGGAR' OR FOOTPADDING 'TRAILER' TO MEET THE ORDER OF A CROOKED DEALER IN THE SOUTH.

IF THE HORSE WERE OF QUALITY, THE DEALER OR 'MARTAR' WOULD GO TO GREAT LENGTHS TO ALTER ITS BRAND AND LOOKS LEST IT BE RECOGNISED WHEN BEING OFFERED TO AN OTHER-WISE UNSUSPECTING BUYER.

LESSER MOUNTS WERE 'CHOPPED OUT' TO THE LOWEST CLASS OF DEALER, THE 'JOCKEY', WHO WOULD THEN SELL THEM ON AT 'BLIND FAYRES' TO THE LESS KNOWLEDGEABLE MEMBERS OF THE PUBLIC.

SINCE THE COACH, EVEN ON THE OUTSIDE, WAS STILL EXPENSIVE, THE PUBLIC WHO HAD TO TRAVEL, PARTICULARLY THE MIDDLE CLASS TRADESMEN, HAD TO RIDE WHETHER THEY WANTED TO OR NOT.

FOR ALL THE UNFORTUNATES WHO WERE NOT INSTINCTIVE HORSEMEN, A CHARLES THOMPSON WROTE THE 'RULES FOR BAD HORSEMEN', OR 'HOW TO GET BY' A BOOK SENSIBLY DESIGNED TO TAKE SOME OF THE AGONY OUT OF THIS 'UTILITY EQUITATION',

AND TREATING RIDING NOT AS AN ART BUT AS A NECESSITY OF LIFE (WHICH IT WAS). IT WAS FULL OF SOUND ADVICE AND GRAPHIC ILLUSTRATIONS OF THE WORKINGS OF THE HORSE : 'A PLANK PLACED IN AEQUILIBRIO CANNOT RISE AT ONE END UNLESS IT SINKS AT THE OTHER'.

LA GUERINIÈRE ON THE OTHER HAND WAS VERY MUCH CONCERNED WITH THE ART OF HORSEMANSHIP, IN MAN'S CONTROL, AND THE GRACE BEAUTY AND POWER OF THE HORSE IN VARIOUS MOVEMENTS SUCH AS THE PIROUETTE, ONE OF THE 'AIRS ON THE GROUND'

AND THE EVEN MORE DRAMATIC 'AIRS ABOVE GROUND' SUCH AS THE 'CROUPADE' AND THE FEARSOME 'CAPRIOLE' WHICH SEES THE HORSE IN MID-AIR DELIVERING A MIGHTY BLOW WITH ITS HIND HOOVES WHILE THE RIDER REMAINS MOTIONLESS.

THESE 'AIRS' CAME OF COURSE DIRECTLY FROM THE TRADITIONAL TRAINING OF THE 'DESTRIER', AND BEING PERFORMED IN A MANEGE OR RING, THEY UNDOUBTEDLY PROVIDED THE INSPIRATION FOR THE MORE LIGHT-HEARTED ENTERTAINMENT OF THE CIRCUS RING.

MEANWHILE NAPOLEON'S HARAHS OF WARHORSES WERE CALLED UPON TO CHALLENGE WELLINGTON'S CAVALRY OF 'GENTLEMEN'S HUNTERS DURING WHICH THE MOST IMPORTANT 'AIR' IN VIEW OF ALL THE ORDNANCE FLYING AROUND WAS THAT DISCOVERED BY THE CAVEMAN.

AFTER ALL THE MAYHEM OF WATERLOO THE HUNTER WAS NO DOUBT GLAD TO CARRY HIS MASTER BACK TO THE PEACE AND TRANQUILITY OF THE COUNTRY ESTATE AND TO THE SAFER PURSUITS OF THE HUNTING FIELD.

AND TO PREPARE FOR THE GOLDEN AGE OF HUNTING, AN AGE WHEN LOOKING GOOD ON THE HORSE, WITH ONE'S SEAT AND TURNOUT, WERE PERHAPS EQUALLY AS IMPORTANT AS BEING ABLE TO CHARGE ACROSS MILES OF MUDDY FIELDS.

WITH THE RETURN OF PEACE ONCE MORE TO EUROPE NOT ALL THE WARHORSES WERE MADE REDUNDANT. THE BEST OF THEM WERE CHOSEN FOR THE ÉLITE CADRE NOIR, AN 'HAUTE ÉCOLE' DEDICATED TO PRESERVING THE CLASSICAL 'AIRS'.

THE REST RETURNED TO WHAT SHOULD HAVE BEEN A MORE PEACEFUL LIFE ON FARM AND ROAD, REJOINING THEIR HEAVIER COUSIN, THE OLD SUMPTER, HELPING TO EVOLVE A WIDE RANGE OF DRAUGHT BREEDS, EACH WITH ITS OWN LITTLE PECULIARITIES.

BUT THE ADVENT OF THE CANAL NETWORKS, ALTHOUGH A SEEMINGLY TRANQUIL AND PEACEFUL OCCUPATION FOR THE DRAUGHT HORSE SUCH AS THE SHIRE, WERE IN FACT AN INDICATOR OF MUCH MORE FRANTIC TIMES TO COME.

THE ABILITY OF THE BARGE-HORSE TO MOVE A WEIGHT OF GOODS THAT HAD PREVIOUSLY TAKEN MANY WAGGONS OR PACKHORSES, WITH APPARENT EASE, STARTED CIVILISATION THINKING OF WAYS OF FURTHER IMPROVEMENT.

THE FIRST RAILWAYS WERE ALSO HORSE-DRAWN BUT IT WAS NOT LONG BEFORE THE NEW STEAM ENGINE HAD BEEN FITTED WITH WHEELS, WHICH RELIEVED THE HORSE OF THE PROBLEM OF WHETHER TO STEP ON OR OFF THE SLEEPERS,

EXCEPT IN SOME AREAS, SUCH AS THE MINES, WHERE THE LOW ENCLOSED SPACES DIDN'T ALLOW FOR ALL THE SMOKE AND STEAM. HERE THE SMALLER NATIVE PONIES WERE HAPPY TO ASSIST MAN IN PRODUCING THE FUEL FOR CIVILISATION'S NEXT GREAT STEP.

WITH THE RAILWAYS IN PLACE THE INDUSTRIAL REVOLUTION HAD TO START IN EARNEST, PRODUCING LOTS OF THINGS TO GIVE THE RAILWAYS SOMETHING TO DO AND TO FURTHER THE SPREAD OF CIVILISATION.

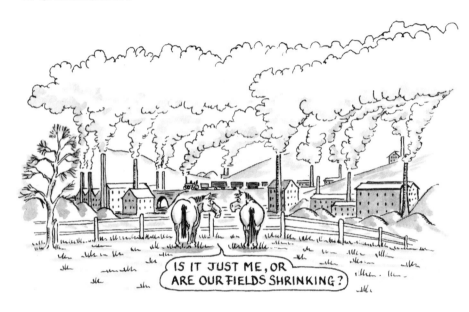

ALTHOUGH BY CARRYING PASSENGERS AS WELL THE RAILWAYS WERE TO MAKE BOTH THE CARTER AND THE MAILCOACH REDUNDANT, CIVILISATION STILL NEEDED THE SERVICES OF THE HORSE IF IT WAS TO GO FORWARD.

WHEN THIS FLOOD OF GOODS AND PASSENGERS REACHED THEIR STATION THEY NEEDED TO BE DISTRIBUTED AND DELIVERED TO THEIR DOORS SINCE CIVILISATION HAD DECIDED THAT WALKING WAS 'NOT DONE' UNLESS THERE WAS NO OTHER CHOICE.

THE COBBLED STREETS BECAME CRAMMED WITH EVERY SORT OF CONVEYANCE; OMNIBUSES AND TRAMS, HANSOMS, GROWLERS AND GIGS, DELIVERY WAGGONS AND VANS ALL JOSTLED FOR SPACE AND IN THE PROCESS INVENTED THE TRAFFIC JAM.

IN A LARGE CITY LIKE LONDON THERE WERE AS MANY AS 300,000 COBS, HACKNEYS AND OTHER HORSES ALL OF WHICH NEEDED TO BE FED AND, IMPORTANTLY, CLEARED UP AFTER. MEN HAD EVEN TO BE EMPLOYED TO SWEEP THE STREET CROSSINGS.

THE ADVANCES IN TRANSPORT AND INCREASING AFFLUENCE AT LAST OPENED UP THE WORLD OF LEISURE TO THE POPULATION AT LARGE, AND ENABLED THEM TO ENJOY SPORTS SUCH AS RACING, SO THE 'JOCKEY' EVOLVED FROM DEALER TO THE DARLING OF THE CROWDS.

AS MORE PEOPLE WERE ABLE TO ENJOY THE THRILL OF THE CHASE SO RULES AND ETIQUETTE WERE INTRODUCED TO HUNTING TO PREVENT THE LARGER 'FIELDS' FROM OVERWHELMING THE MASTER AND TRAMPLING HOUNDS.

POLO WAS INTRODUCED FROM INDIA, WHERE IT HAD EVOLVED FROM 'SAVLAJAM' A VARIETY OF THE STEPPES GAME OF 'TCHIGAN' A DANGEROUS FORM OF MOUNTED TENNIS.

REMARKABLY IT HAD TAKEN LESS THAN TWO HUNDRED YEARS FOR
THE NORTH AMERICAN INDIAN TO CATCH UP WITH THEIR ANCIENT COUSINS
FROM THE STEPPES IN THE ART OF AGGRESSIVE HORSEMANSHIP — AND
THEREBY GIVING THE INVADING WHITEMAN A HARD TIME.

BUT SINCE ACQUIRING THE 'MEDICINE DOG' FROM THE EARLY SETTLERS
AND THE ESCAPEE 'MESTENGO' OR MUSTANG ONLY THE NEZ PERCE HAD
BOTHERED TO SELECTIVELY BREED THE HORSE (THE APPALOOSA), THE
REST DIDN'T MIND AS LONG AS THEY HAD FOUR HOOVES AND WERE 'PAINTS'

THIS INDISCRIMINATE BREEDING LED TO ALL SORTS OF 'PAINTS', OF PINTOS, PIEBALDS, SKEWBALDS, ODDBALDS AND OTHER 'CAYUSES', BUT WHILE THEY WERE NO MATCH FOR THE CAREFULLY BRED MOUNTS OF THE WHITEMAN, THEIR NATURAL CAMOUFLAGE HAD DEFINITE ADVANTAGES.

IF IN DOUBT, HIDE!

THE SHORT-LIVED PONY EXPRESS, EMULATING THE PERSIAN, GREEK AND MONGOL COURIERS, RELIED ON THE QUALITY OF MOUNT TO CARRY THE MAILS 2000 MILES TO SACRAMENTO THROUGH FLOOD, BLIZZARD, AVALANCHE AND HOSTILE INDIANS IN JUST EIGHT DAYS.

YOU'RE TWO MINUTES LATE! WHAT KEPT YOU??

SACRAMENTO

BUT IN THE SPACE OF TWO YEARS THE HARD-RIDING DUO WITH THEIR PRECIOUS SATCHEL OF URGENT MESSAGES WERE BEING OVER-TAKEN BY THE DEMANDS OF CIVILISATION FOR SPEED AND RELIAB-ILITY, IN THE SHAPE OF THE 'SINGING WIRE' OR TELEGRAPH,

AND BY THE RELIABILITY OF THE STAGE COACH, WHICH, WHILE IT ONLY COVERED 125 MILES A DAY COULD CARRY A HEAVY LOAD OF PASSENGERS AND PARCELS THROUGH THE WORST OF THE ELE-MENTS STILL QUICKLY ENOUGH TO OUTRUN THE HAZARDS.

WHILE THE CAVALRY WAS MOSTLY SUCCESSFUL AT KEEPING CIVIL-
ISATION'S LINES OF COMMUNICATION OPEN, THEY DIDN'T, DESPITE THE
SUPERIORITY OF THEIR HORSES (AND OVERALL NUMBERS), ALWAYS
HAVE IT ALL THEIR OWN WAY.

AND IT WAS THE ARRIVAL OF THE 'IRON HORSE' THAT FINALLY SEALED
THE FATE OF THE INDIANS. THE RAILWAYS ENCOURAGED THE ELIMINATION
OF THE BUFFALO SINCE THEY KNEW THE 'HOSTILES' COULD NOT EXIST WITH-
OUT IT, BESIDES, THE HUGE HERDS CREATED HAVOC WITH TIMETABLES.

WITH THE DEPARTURE OF THE LAST OF THE 'HOSTILES' UNDER SITTING BULL TO THE 'LAND OF THE GRANDMOTHER' (CANADA) IT WAS LEFT TO THE COWBOY TO CONTINUE AMERICA'S CLOSE ASSOCIATION WITH THE HORSE.

IN SOUTH AMERICA THE DESCENDENT'S OF PIZARRO'S HERDSMEN, THE GAUCHOS, KEPT FAITH WITH THE OFFSPRING OF THE ANDALUSIAN RIDDEN BY THEIR FOREFATHERS. THE 'CRIOLLO' WAS A FAST AGILE WORKHORSE THAT WAS TO PROVE IDEAL FOR MOUNTED GAMES.

IN AUSTRALIA THE ABORIGINE PEOPLE, LIKE THE NORTH AM-
ERICAN INDIAN, SHOWED A REMARKABLE NATURAL FLAIR WITH
THE HORSE AND LOST NO TIME IN CATCHING UP WITH THEIR WHITE
COUNTERPARTS IN THE DEMANDING ART OF STOCKMANSHIP.

IN NEW ZEALAND THE MAORIS PROVED TO BE JUST AS SKILLFUL
WITH THE HORSE ALTHOUGH THE RUGGED TERRAIN AND CLIMATE DEM-
ANDED A WIDER RANGE OF SKILLS OF THE STOCKMAN THERE, SUCH AS
BEING ABLE TO SAIL EFFORTLESSLY OVER OBSTACLES — EVEN WATER!

IN SOUTH AFRICA THE BOER 'VOORTREKKERS' HAD MORE THAN JUST STOCKMANSHIP AND THE TERRAIN TO WORRY ABOUT, HUGELY OUTNUMBERED BY WELL-ORGANISED 'IMPIS' OR REGIMENTS, OF ZULU WARRIORS THEY RESORTED TO THE PARTHIAN TACTICS OF HIT AND RUN;

A TACTIC THAT NOT ONLY DEFEATED THE ZULU BUT ALSO BROUGHT THEM INTO CONFLICT WITH THE BRITISH AND GAVE THE BRITISH INFANTRY A HARD TIME AS WELL, UNTIL COMMON SENSE PREVAILED AND PEACE BROKE OUT.

THE BRITISH HAD GONE OFF CAVALRY SOMEWHAT SINCE THE DISASTROUS OCCASION IN THE CRIMEAN CAMPAIGN WHEN THE LIGHT BRIGADE HAPPENED TO CHOOSE THE SAME VALLEY TO EXERCISE IN THAT THE RUSSIAN GUNNERS HAD BOOKED FOR TARGET PRACTISE.

AND IT WAS LEFT TO COUNTRIES SUCH AS PRUSSIA, POLAND AND RUSSIA TO MAINTAIN LARGE CAVALRY FORMATIONS WHILE THE BRITISH DECIDED TO KEEP THEIRS FOR DISPLAY AND FOR CERE-MONIAL OCCASIONS.

THE HORSE WAS NOW NOT ONLY AN ESSENTIAL PART OF EVERY-DAY LIFE IT WAS ALSO A CRUCIAL PART OF THE SOCIAL SCENE, WHEN TO RIDE INDIFFERENTLY OR 'INCORRECTLY' WAS TO BE COMPLETELY BEYOND THE SOCIAL PALE .

WHILE THERE WERE OF COURSE THOSE FORTUNATES, PERHAPS BORN INTO LAND-OWNING HUNTING FAMILIES, TO WHOM HORSEMAN-SHIP WAS SOMETHING AS NATURAL AS BLOOD AND WHO WERE IN THE SADDLE BEFORE THEY COULD WALK ,

THERE WERE MANY OTHERS, ASPIRING TO GREATER SOCIAL HEIGHTS WHO NEEDED THE WORDS OF WISDOM OF THE MANY EXPERTS SUCH AS JAMES FILLIS'S 'DRESSAGE ET EQUITATION'. ALTHOUGH, AS ITS ENGLISH TITLE (BREAKING AND RIDING) CONFIRMS, IT WASN'T ALL ABOUT DRESSAGE,

BUT SEEMINGLY CONCERNED ITSELF MORE WITH THE SIDE—SADDLE BEING THE ONLY WAY FOR A LADY TO RIDE WITHOUT COMING OFF AND THE IMPORTANCE OF THE FIT OF HER MANY GARMENTS FOR HER COMFORT AND PEACE OF MIND WHEN RIDING.

FEDERICO CAPRILLI ON THE OTHER HAND PRODUCED A LASTING NEW DOCTRINE: 'ACCOMPANYING WITH THE BODY THE FORWARD THRUST OF THE CENTRE OF GRAVITY', WHICH WAS DISCOVERED BY STUDYING THE RIDERLESS HORSE JUMPING.

THIS 'FORWARD SEAT' DOCTRINE DEPENDED ON NOT 'GIVING THE OFFICE' WHEN JUMPING BUT ALLOWING THE HORSE HIS HEAD AND KEEPING THE INTERFERENCE TO A MINIMUM WHILE STILL GUARDING AGAINST HIM 'PUTTING IN A SHORT ONE'.

BUT IF THE 'FORWARD SEAT' WAS TO FORM THE BASIS FOR MODERN COMPETITION, SOCIAL RIDING WAS PURELY CONCERNED WITH CUTTING A DASH IN THE CLASSICAL STYLE. IT WAS ENOUGH JUST TO LOOK GOOD ON THE HORSE SINCE THERE WERE NO JUMPS IN THE LIKES OF ROTTEN ROW.

MANY HUNTS TOO WERE BECOMING MORE CONCERNED WITH QUALITY OF TURNOUT THAN QUALITY OF JUMPING. IT WAS EVEN POSSIBLE TO TRAVEL YOUR ENTOURAGE OF SPARE MOUNTS, GROOMS ETC. TO THE MEET BY TRAIN TO AVOID SPOILING THE PRESENTATION WITH A MUDDY HACK.

THROUGH ALL THIS GREAT LEAP OF CIVILISATION TRUE HORSE-
MANSHIP REMAINED A 'MAGIC CIRCLE' RELUCTANT TO ADMIT OUT-
SIDERS. IT WAS FULL OF CLOSELY GUARDED ANCIENT ARTS LIKE THE
'JADING' OF A HORSE OR THE STOPPING OF IT IN ITS TRACKS.

ACKNOWLEDGED AND RESPECTED BY ALL STRATA OF SOCIETY, THE
HIGH PRIEST OF THE HORSE KNEW NOT ONLY HOW TO 'JADE' BUT, MORE
IMPORTANTLY, ALL THE SECRET POTIONS THAT WOULD ENABLE HIM
TO 'DRAW' ANY HORSE TO HIM.

DESPITE ALL THE PEACE ABOUT, HORSEMANSHIP WAS STILL VERY MUCH MILITARY-ORIENTATED. IT WAS IN FACT THE PRUSSIAN CAVALRY THAT HELD THE FIRST MODERN EQUESTRIAN COMPETITION (APART FROM RACING) A SORT OF ROADS AND TRACKS – ONLY IT WAS OVER 580 KM!

THE LAST AND GREATEST CHANGE IN CIVILISATION'S RELATION-SHIP WITH THE HORSE WAS, LIKE THE RAILWAY ENGINE USHERED IN BY A CLOUD OF SMOKE, DUST AND NOISE, AND WAS ALSO PRECEDED BY A MAN WITH A RED FLAG.

THEN CAME CIVILISATION'S FIRST SERIOUS ATTEMPT TO SELF-DESTRUCT. ALTHOUGH CAVALRY WAS STILL DEPLOYED ON THE EASTERN FRONT, THE HORSE ON THE WESTERN FRONT WAS CONFINED TO 'PACK-HORSING' SUPPLIES SINCE THE CONDITIONS WERE TOO BAD FOR THE 'CAR'.

BUT BY THE END OF THE MADNESS, IMPROVEMENTS TO THE 'HORSELESS-CARRIAGE' OR 'CAR' ALLOWED IT TO MOVE WHERE IT WANTED, REGARDLESS OF CONDITIONS, WHICH HAPPILY RELIEVED THE HORSE OF THE DEMEANING AND RETROGRADE STEP.

FOLLOWING IN THE TRACKS OF THE TANK CAME THE TRACTOR, THE HORSELESS CARRIAGE THAT WOULD FINALLY RELIEVE THE HEAVY HORSE OF THE DRUDGERY OF PLODDING UP AND DOWN FIELDS AND FREE TO DO MORE ESSENTIAL THINGS LIKE PULLING BREWERY DRAYS.

DUE TO CIVILISATION'S OBSESSION WITH SPEED THE 'CAR' SOON BECAME GENERALLY ACCEPTED EVEN TO THE EXTENT OF THE LIFTING OF THE 20 M.P.H. SPEED LIMIT IMPOSED ON THE 'INFERNAL' COMBUST-ION ENGINE THUS ALLOWING IT TO GO FASTER THAN A COACH AND PAIR.

IN A FEW SHORT MOMENTOUS YEARS THE UBIQUITOUS ENGINE WAS DOING EVERYTHING OF IMPORTANCE ONCE DONE BY THE HORSE AND THE HORSE'S RELATIONSHIP WITH CIVILISATION CHANGED DRAMATICALLY FROM THAT OF SERVANT TO THAT OF FRIEND.

WHAT THE ENGINE COULD NOT DO WAS RECAPTURE 5000 YEARS OF EXCITEMENT AND DANGER, 5000 YEARS IN WHICH THE HORSE HAD BEEN ALL-IMPORTANT, 5000 YEARS WHICH HAD SEEN THE HORSE AND MAN PROGRESS SO FAR.

IT COULD HOWEVER ENABLE MORE AND MORE PEOPLE TO RE-
LIVE THOSE PAST CONFLICTS IN THE MANY AND VARIED FORMS
OF EQUESTRIAN COMPETITION THAT WERE EVOLVING – A SORT
OF 'PALFREY' ON WHEELS FOR THE KNIGHT AND HIS 'DESTRIER'.

ABOUT THE ONLY GOOD THING TO EMERGE FROM THE SECOND
WORLD WAR (FROM AN EQUESTRIAN POINT OF VIEW) WAS THE FOUR
WHEEL DRIVE VEHICLE. NOW LOTS MORE PEOPLE COULD ENJOY THE CH-
ALLENGE OF NEGOTIATING THE AVERAGE COMPETITION VEHICLE PARK.

ALTHOUGH NOT EXACTLY COMPETITION (EXCEPT IN ONEUPMAN-SHIP!) HUNTING STILL TAKES US BACK THOSE 5000 YEARS TO A TIME WHEN DANGER LURKED AROUND AND SURVIVAL DEPENDED ABOVE ALL ON THE COURAGEOUS HORSE.

FROM HUNTING CAME JUMPING IN AN ARENA. ALTHOUGH THE FIRST SHOW JUMPING COMPETITION (THE OLYMPICS) WERE STILL MILITARY DOMINATED, IT SOON BECAME HUGELY POPULAR, ALLOWING ALL TO PIT THEIR COURAGE AGAINST OTHERS IN FRIENDLY RIVALRY.

RACING, WITH ITS ANCIENT HERITAGE, CONTINUES TO ENJOY GREAT SUPPORT EVEN THOUGH PARTICIPATION FOR MOST IS CONFINED TO WATCHING AND PERHAPS BEING LUCKY ENOUGH TO COLLECT THEIR WINNINGS ON A SUCCESSFUL BET.

DRESSAGE, ALTHOUGH NOT SO POPULAR (PARTICULARLY WITH THE HORSE!) TRACES ITS ORIGINS BACK TO THE TRAINING OF THE WARHORSE AND THE HAUTE ÉCOLE, HOWEVER NOWADAYS THE 'AIRS' ARE SOMEWHAT TONED DOWN AND ARE CONFINED TO THOSE 'ON THE GROUND'.

'LONG DISTANCE' IS A REMINDER OF THE HUGE DISTANCES THAT HAD TO BE COVERED BY THE CAVALRY WHEN ON CAMPAIGN AND NOW GIVES BOTH RIDER AND HORSE A CHANCE TO TEST THEIR RESILIENCE IN SOME OF THE WILDER AND MORE REMOTE AREAS OF THE COUNTRYSIDE.

TRIALS AND EVENTING REACH THEIR PINACLE IN THE THREE DAY EVENT WHICH REQUIRES ALL THE DISCIPLINES: DRESSAGE, ROADS AND TRACKS, RACING, CROSS COUNTRY AND SHOW JUMPING, AND WHICH DEMANDS THE GREATEST FITNESS AND DEDICATION OF ANY COMPETITION.

POLO, BROUGHT OVER FROM INDIA, IS MOST EXCLUSIVE AND THRILLS THE CROWDS WITH ITS AURA OF PAST CLOSE COMBAT AND SHOWS OFF TO PERFECTION THE POLO PONY'S REMARKABLE SKILLS OF AGILITY AND ACCELERATION.

AND IT WAS THE CROSSING OF THE POLO PONY WITH THE SMALLER NATIVES THAT PRODUCED THE IDEAL MOUNT FOR CHILDREN TO BE ABLE TO START COMPETING AT GYMKHANAS AND TO MAKE A VERSATILE COMPANION TO SHARE IN THE VARIED ACTIVITIES OF PONY CLUB CAMP.

DRIVING ALSO REQUIRES GREAT VERSATILITY FROM THE HORSE WHEN PULLING A VARIETY OF VEHICLES IN COMPETITIONS INVOLVING NOT JUST TURNOUT BUT ALSO DRESSAGE, SCURRY AND MARATHON OR CROSS COUNTRY THEREBY GIVING US AN EDUCATIONAL AND NOSTALGIC GLIMPSE OF THE PAST.

BUT ABOVE ALL, ALTHOUGH NOT COMPETITION, IT IS PERHAPS THE SIMPLE HACK THAT EPITOMISES CIVILISATION'S NEW RELAT- IONSHIP WITH THE HORSE - AS A FRIEND TO SHARE IN THE QUIET PLEASURES, THE SIGHTS AND SOUNDS OF THE COUNTRYSIDE.

INDEED EVEN TODAY'S 'WORKING HORSE' IS AN ESSENTIAL PART OF CIVILISATION'S HARD-WON LEISURE, A FRIEND WHO DEMONSTRATES OUR HISTORY WITH JOUSTING AND PLOUGHING, WHO HEADS STATE OCCASIONS AND EVEN LENDS A BENEVOLENT PRESENCE TO CROWD CONTROL.

AND IF ANY REMINDER WERE NECESSARY OF THE IMPORTANCE OF OUR FRIEND IN HISTORY, THE FILMS, FROM GREEK EPIC TO WESTERN, SHOULD LEAVE US IN NO DOUBT THAT IN CIVILISATION'S PAINFUL PROGRESS TOWARDS THE SUNLIT UPLANDS, IT IS THE HORSE THAT HAS BEEN THE STAR!

ANDSO AFTER ALL THE HORSE'S EFFORTS TO GET MANKIND THIS FAR, AND AFTER ALL THAT THE HORSE HAS BEEN THROUGH IN CIVILIS-ATION'S SERVICE IN ITS CONSTANT BATTLES TO SURVIVE AND GO FORWARD, IT IS RIGHT AND PROPER THAT THE ROLES SHOULD NOW BE REVERSED AND CIVILISATION SHOULD SHOW ITS APPRECIATION BY TREASURING THE HORSE, FORGIVING THE HORSE THE LITTLE PHOBIAS AND FOIBLES ACQUIRED IN THOSE 5000 ODD YEARS AND MAKE SURE THAT THE HORSE'S EVERY LITTLE NEED IS ATTENDED TO.